Bedtime Chess A Rook Story
Copyright © 2021 by Daniel Hallback
All Rights Reserved.

No part of this book may be used or reproduced by any means, graphic, electronic, or mechanical, including photocopying, recording, taping, or by any information storage retrieval system without the written permission of the publisher except in the case of brief quotations embodied in critical articles and reviews.
ISBN 978-1955364058

Vets Publish
www.vetspublish.com

Bedtime Chess
A Rook Story

Written By: Daniel Hallback

Little one, it is time for bed.
You have an important day tomorrow.

What is happening tomorrow?

Tomorrow, you will play a game with your friends.

You will play as a rook.

You and your friends will all be on the same team.

The game is called Chess.
It will take place on a chessboard.
There are six different chess pieces:

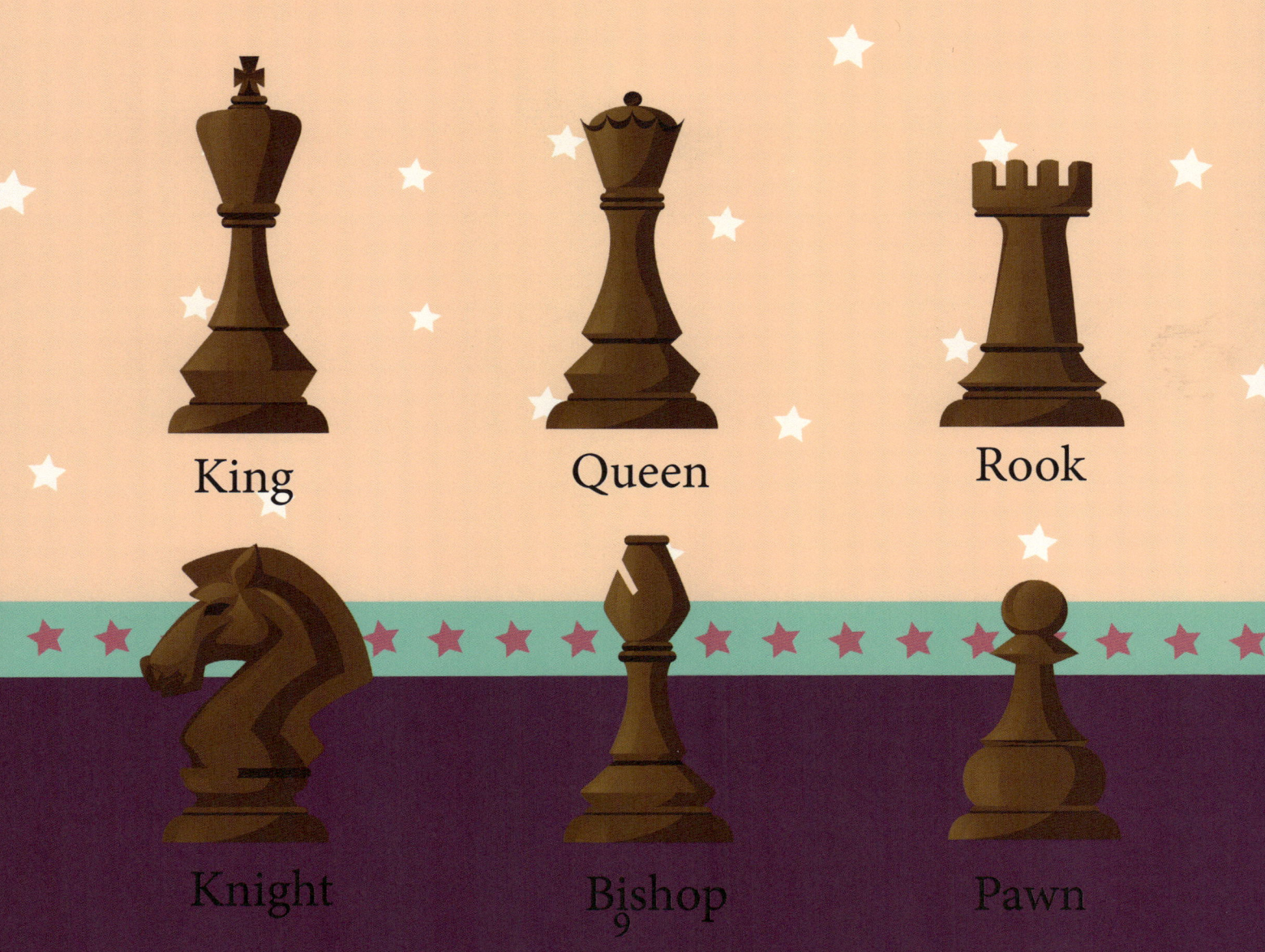

King Queen Rook

Knight Bishop Pawn

You will be one of the two rooks on your team.

Each team will take turns moving one piece across the board.

Rook Moves

- The Rooks each start on one of the four corners of the chessboard.
- They move in a straight line, each move is at least one square and up to 7 squares.
- The rook can not hop over pieces like it's neighbor the knight.

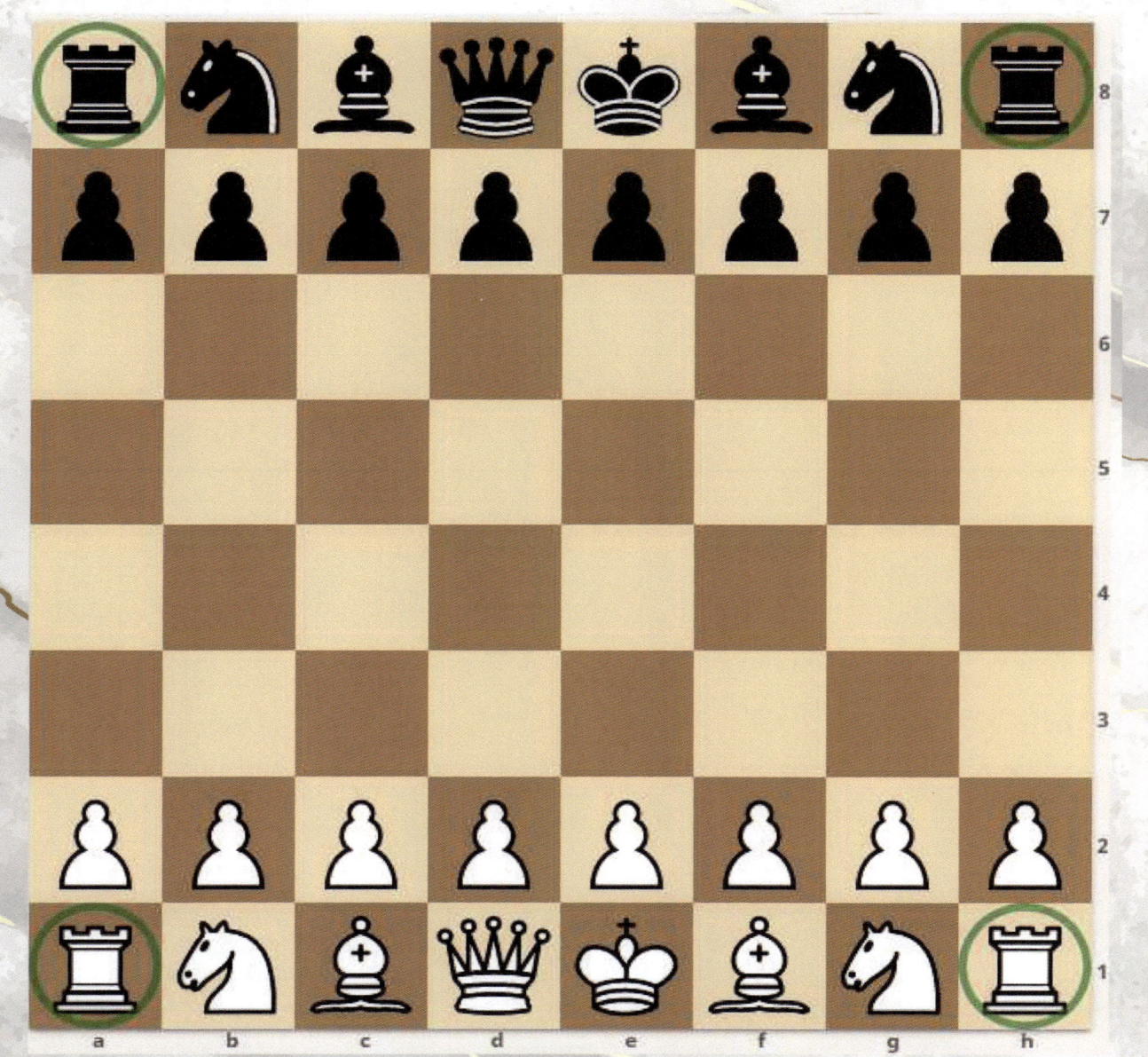

The 4 rooks begin the game in the four corners of the chessboard. They will always start the game next to the a knight

Can the rook capture other pieces?

Good Question !
If an opponent's piece is in the way of the rook.

- The rook can take its square.
- The rook can not pass over the piece, it takes the square and the other piece leaves the board.
- If your teammates are in your way, you have to wait for them to move so that you will be able to move too.

Castling

The rook does have a special move!! It is called castling.

The move is done with the king as a special move where the king moves two spaces towards the king and the king moves two spaces toward the rook.

The king hops over the rook. This helps the king to be safe. It also allows the rook to both protect the king and also be ready to move to attack the opponents king and other pieces.

Castling sounds fun!

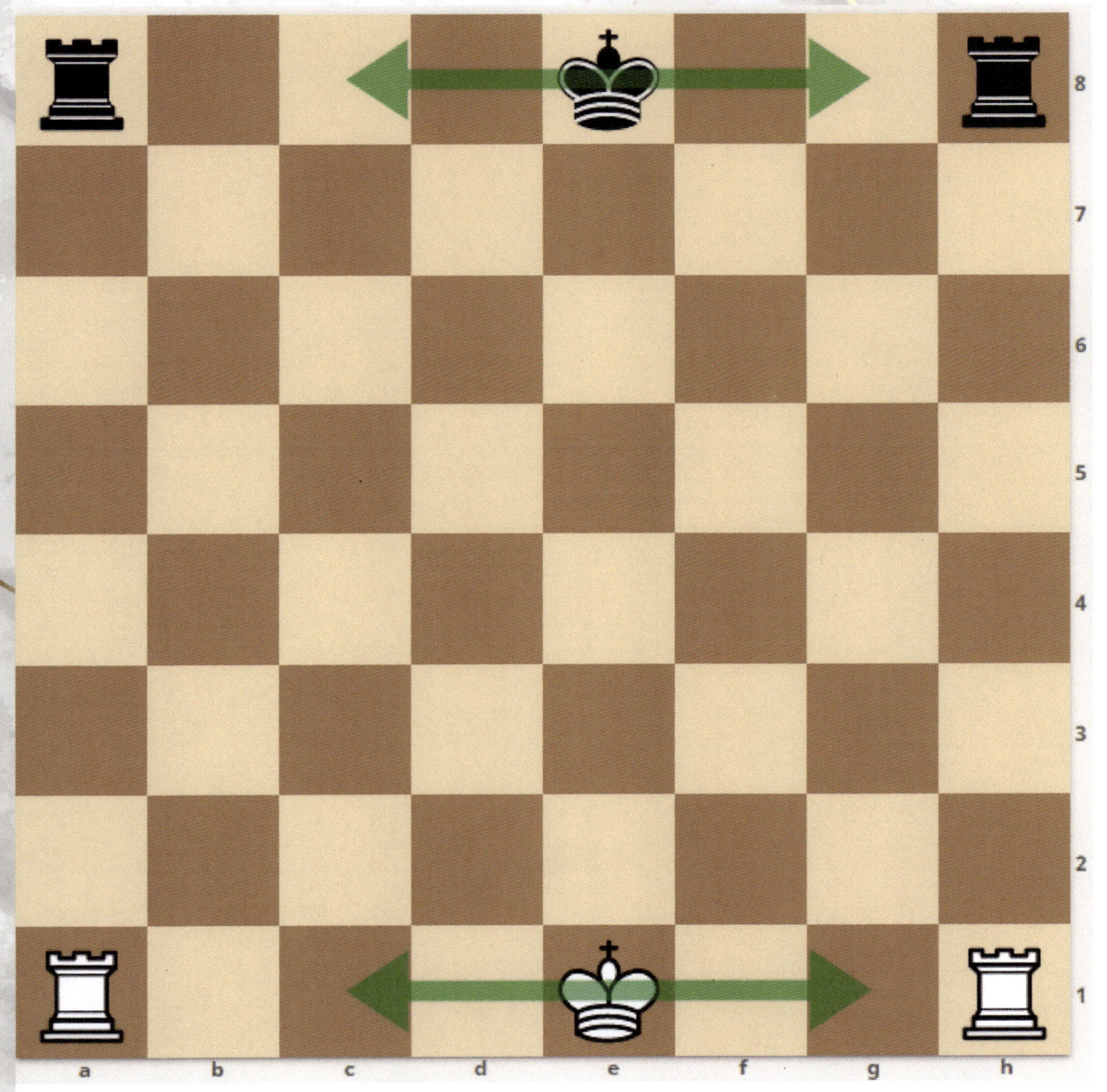

If the King or the Rook has not moved they can castle. You can castle to left which is called kingside castling or castle to the queenside which is called queen side castling.

Castle Queenside

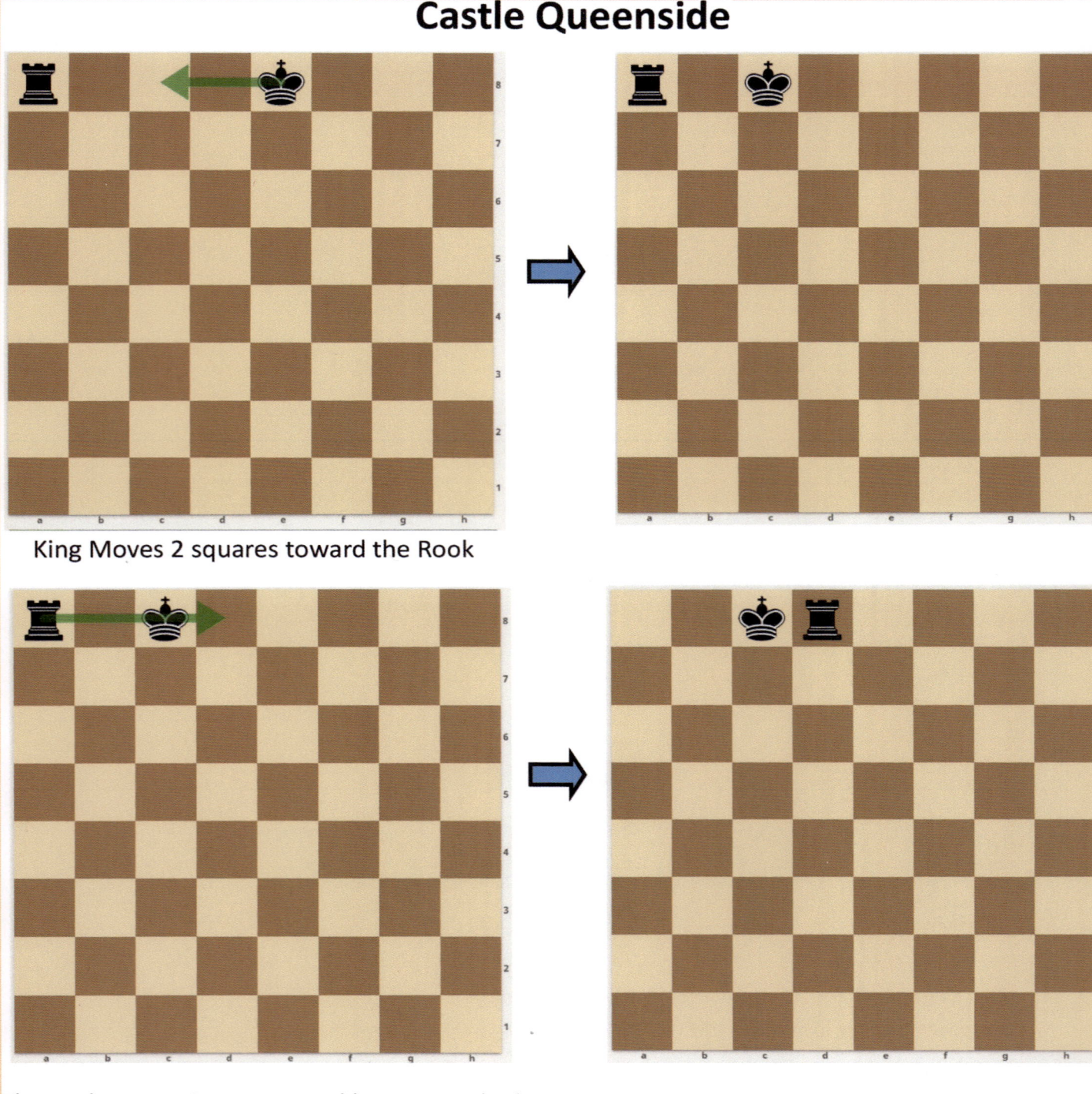

King Moves 2 squares toward the Rook

The rook moves 3 squares and hops over the king

Castle Kingside

King Moves 2 squares toward the Rook

The rook moves 2 squares and hops over the king

Remember that you are a part of a team. You only win if your team wins together. It is important to move together and work with your teammates.

The goal is to checkmate the other team.

I thought that you said that the rook can not hop?

You listen well little one!
This is a special occasion.

It is important to remember that it can only be done as both the first move for the king and rook.

The king also can not be under attack or move through attack to do this.

Is one rook better than the other rook?

Think of them as equals !

Connected Rooks

When they start the game they have 6 of their teammates on the squares between them.

Later in the game when they don't have any pieces in between they are called
"Connected Rooks"

Connected rooks work very well together as both attackers and defenders.

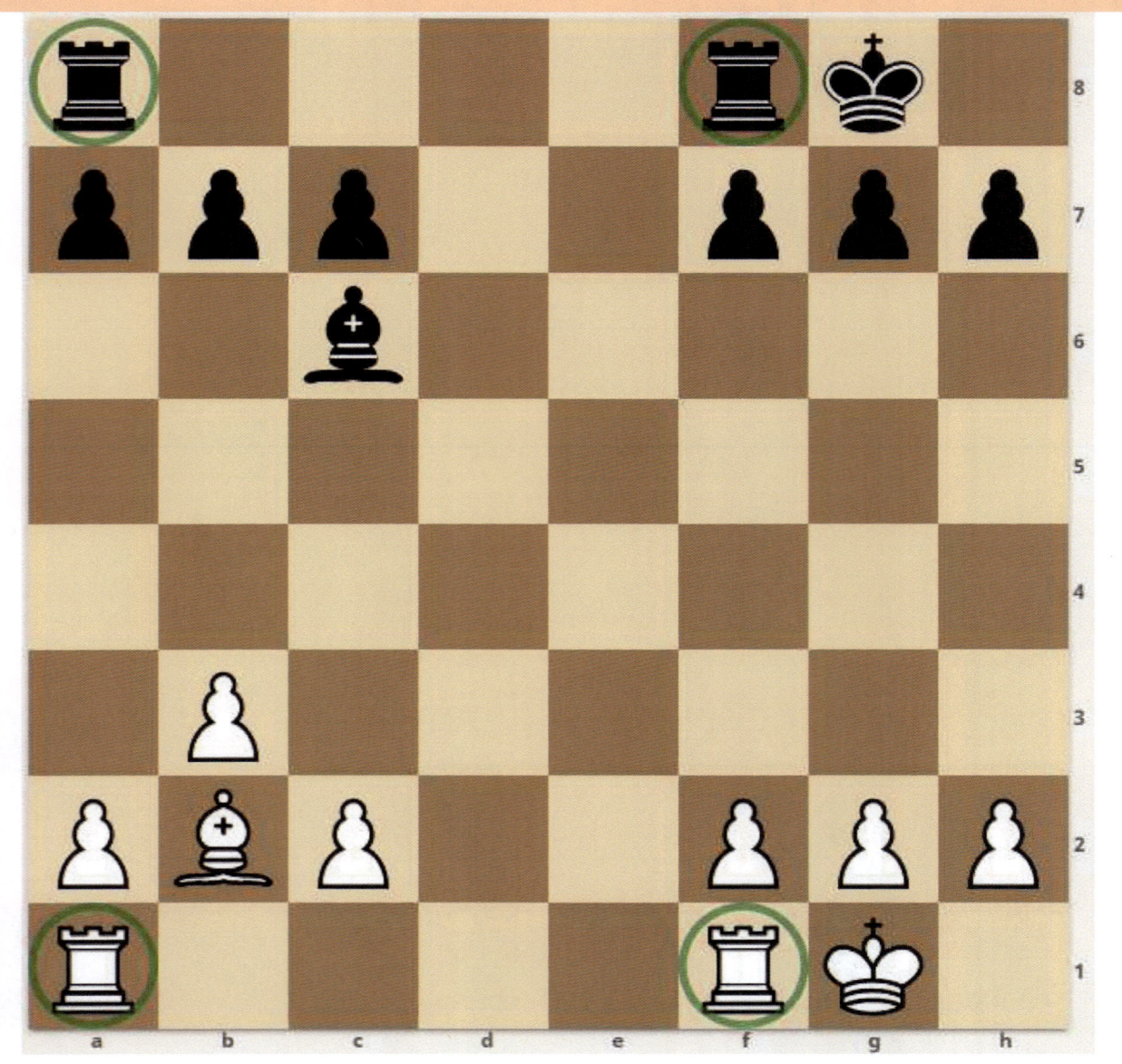

Both sets of rooks are "connected" because there are no pieces between their partner rook.

I hope my team wins!

I want to go to sleep now so that I can be a Rook tomorrow.

"Good Night"

Check out the other Bedtime Chess Books
Bedtime Chess A Pawn Story
Bedtime Chess A Knight Story
Bedtime Chess A Bishop Story
Bedtime Chess A Queen Story
Bedtime Chess A King Story

Please consider leaving a review on Amazon, GoodReads or your site of choice.

Printed in Great Britain
by Amazon